I0786121

falling in love alone

malia nahinu

this book is dedicated to everyone who has fallen in love alone. i hope this brings you as much healing as it has brought to me.

contents

part one: soul searching
page 5

part two: souls meeting
page 26

part three: souls parting
page 48

part four: soul's madness
page 64

part five: soul's wisdom
page 95

part one

soul searching

i just need a quiet place
to collect my thoughts.
they're all over the map.
maybe, if I sit next to
these pine trees long enough
the sentences will come back to me
and life will start to make
sense again.

what is enlightening about
falling in love?
can anyone tell me what
it means?
what is its importance?
i've been fine without it.

i feel
like
i am
missing
parts
of me.
like there
are pieces
of me
i haven't
discovered
yet.

i am sitting in a
building of millionaires
wondering about
their lifestyles
asking myself
if that's what I need
to feel satisfied.

she wanders
the earth
wondering about
her salvations
curious of death
but thirsty for life

have you ever
looked at the night sky,
stared out to the moon long
enough to see just for a moment,
you swear you could see a smile?
then, reality hits you,
like a blizzard,
impossible nothings
mixed in with possible somethings
and you realize your mind is
running away again.

i wish the grass could
steal my worries.
i wish the
soil could
bury
my
regrets.

i took four
sleeping pills again,
just hoping for
a bit of rest
but, instead I am
dreaming about
green monsters
with giant swords
slashing at my
empty wallet,
demanding
payment
for my
existence.

when I am lonely,
i drive to high
mountain tops
to stare
out into the
magenta sunset.

i remember
back to simpler times.

i picture myself naked
to the world,
like a blank canvas
to a painter,
waiting for a great artist
to make their mark.

i feel
i am left in the air
like a let go of balloon,
floating
away
into the sky.

if a leaf fell
into my palm,
i would
pray it keeps
falling
far away
from here,
hope it carries
my wishes
in the winds.

what are we all
searching for
if love doesn't have
plans with us?

some people are so brave,
they smile at people
they've never met before.

i have a hard time smiling
at people I've known for years.

i'm staring at visitor name tags
and I can't stop thinking about
how we are all visitors too.

i sit at a desk
here and there,
seems like
everywhere,
but, usually,
i tend to feel
like
i am always
stuck
in
nowhere.

do you ever go through the day
and not speak?
you just listen to the world
around you,
wondering about some
greater meaning,
convincing yourself
that maybe the more
quiet you become,
the louder
life's answers will sound?

love was
never something
i grew up fantasizing about.
it was always
this Hollywood movie
that the rich and beautiful
got to exist in

i tend to walk
around
near the ocean
staring at the waves
splash at the
rocks,
trying to force
myself to
meditate,
but, ultimately just
sitting in
the silence
splashing
my thoughts
around my mind
with the ocean.

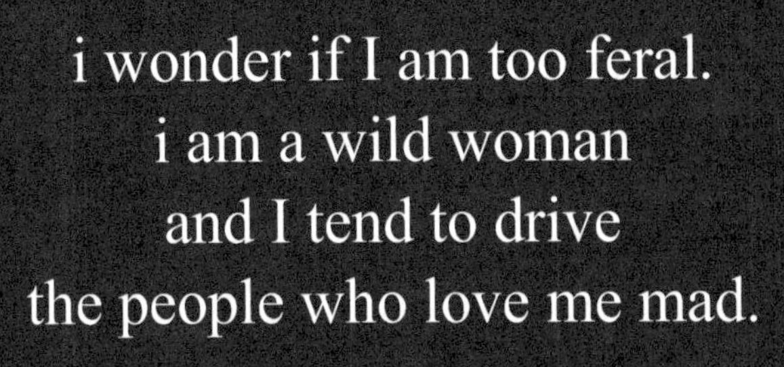
i wonder if I am too feral.
i am a wild woman
and I tend to drive
the people who love me mad.

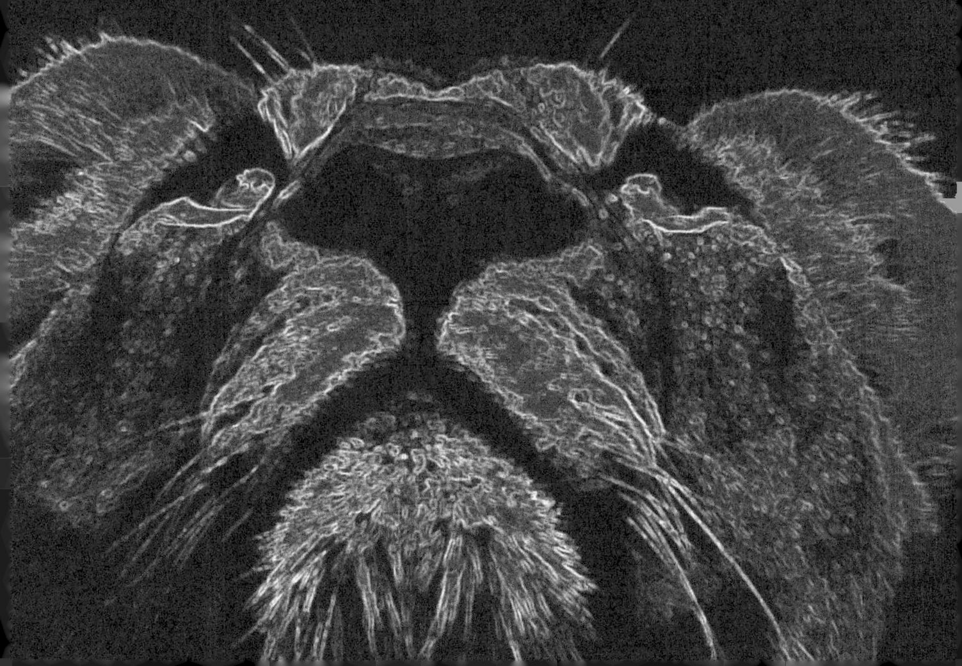

part two

souls meeting

the moment I saw him
my heart blew up.

it was like my entire life had
just been one boring stage play
on autopilot,
the same old dialogue
over and over,
but,
when I saw him
suddenly, the play exploded
into a theatrical masterpiece
with dancing,
with singing,
and drums,
and fireworks,
and laughter,
and joy,
and brilliant choirs,
and stupendous scenery.

the moment I saw him
i knew
nothing could ever be the same,
nothing would ever be the same.

the way he crinkles
his eyebrows
before he smiles
is a sight
more tranquil
than the setting sun.

he is
a déjà vu
he is
a
rainbow
hue
he is
a sweet melon
dew
he is
a wanderlust
view
he is
a foreign escape
he is a dream
awake

he is
a painted
portrait
of Elysian
divinity,
a holy
masculinity.

i wasn't aware
how empty
my heart
was
until I
met
him.

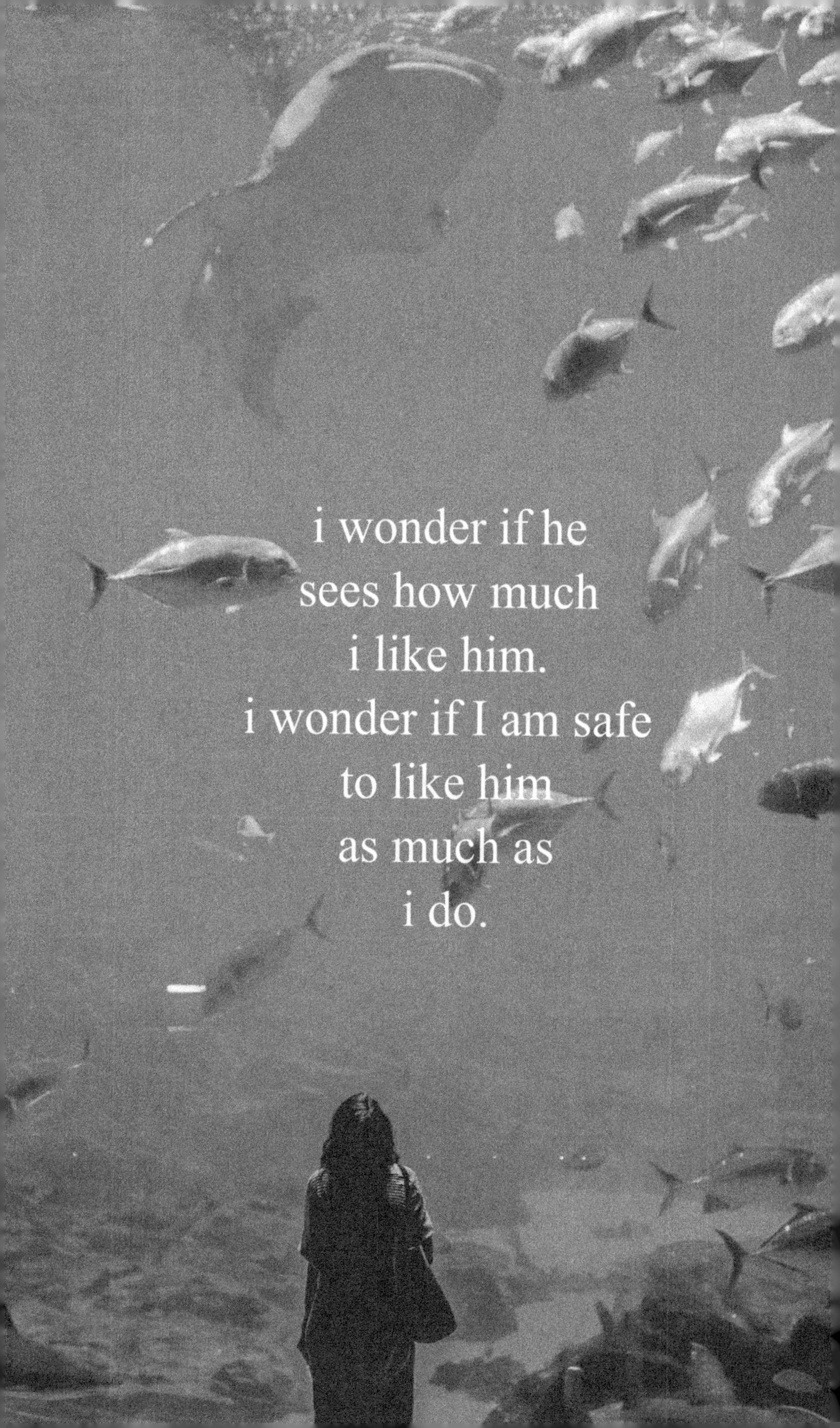

i wonder if he
sees how much
i like him.
i wonder if I am safe
to like him
as much as
i do.

i feel numb.
i can't tell if
it was the drugs
or the alcohol
that blinded me from my
feelings of him for a few days,
but, suddenly
i was hit by a bigger drug.
one that slammed me into
a psychedelic realm
of bliss, irrational hope,
never-ending butterflies,
a yearning,
a need for his honey.

i
feel
addicted
to a human
being
with no
logical
explanation.
i have become
a vampire for
his presence,
and that
terrifies me.

when he held my hand
i felt like rain in the summer
peaceful warmth,
a petrifying
clarity
maybe,
this is *love*.

he told me about his hell
and it made me want
to give him heaven.

he is blue rain,
a miracle appearing
out of the blue
invigorating my
parched heart
with tropical
phenomena
and oceanic
fantasies.

every day
we speak
life
is worth
living.

he put his head on my shoulder
and I could feel the way
he felt like he was home.
I could feel his soul
join into mine
and we both agreed,
this is our home.

you're the
light
my dear
delicate beauty,
a chandelier
pining,
a transient
dream.

i feel I am on top
of the world,
i feel I can do anything,
i feel I am the
luckiest person alive
to be able to
feel this love
it's changing my life.

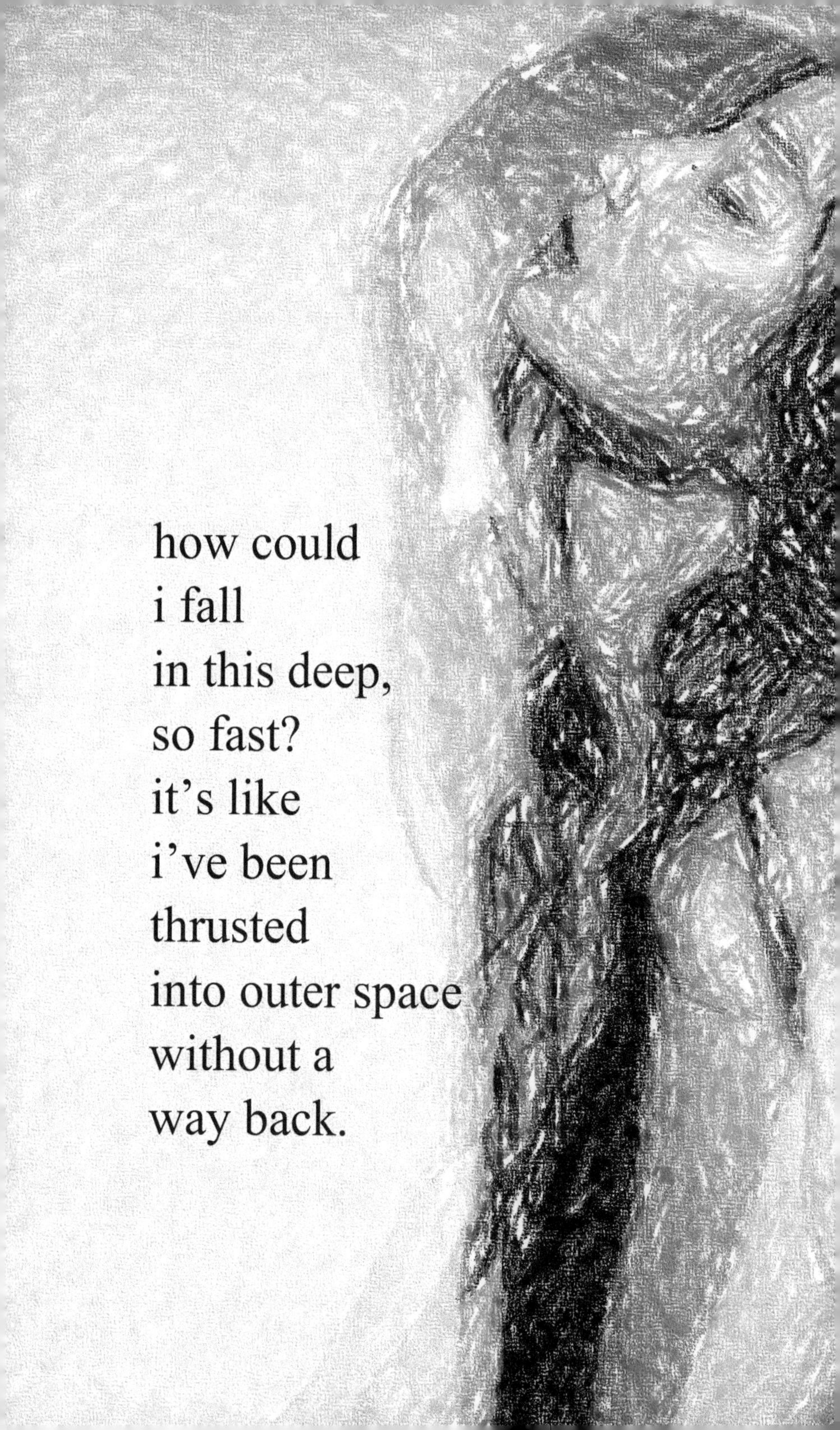
how could
i fall
in this deep,
so fast?
it's like
i've been
thrusted
into outer space
without a
way back.

i
yearn
no more
a life spent
wandered,
i spend
my breaths
in love
less
pondered.

i saw a vision
of our future.
it showed me happiness,
and I called it Hope.
i called you Hope.

i wonder if he feels it too,
the way that I do.

i am a fool for you,
a silly girl in love,
but, I fear
i am losing my mind.

you are my kryptonite.
i am weak to you
and you know it.

part three

souls parting

he
stopped
calling.

he left me on read.

i wonder
what
i said
to mess
everything
up.

i wonder
if this
was all just
my imagination.

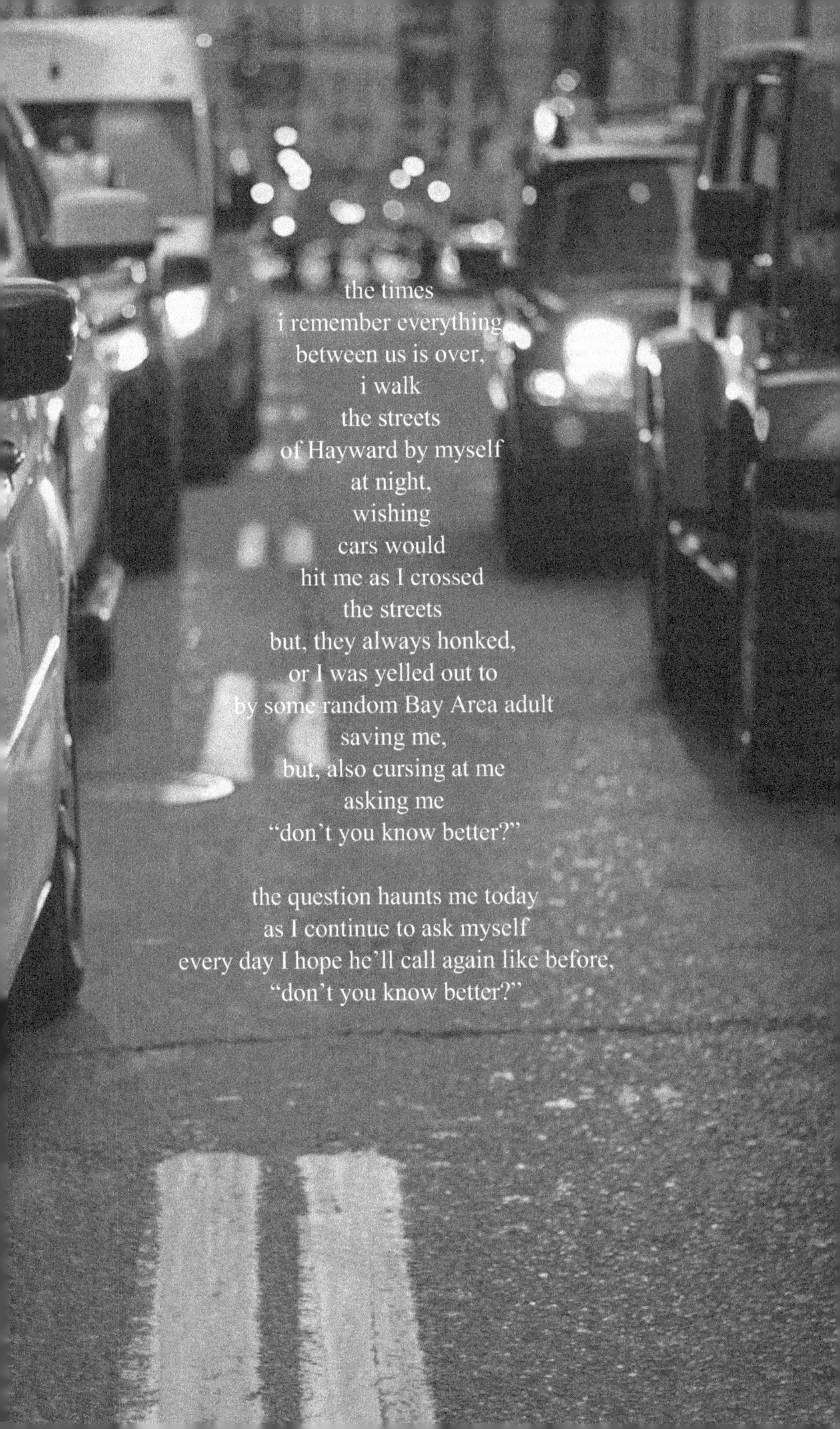

the times
i remember everything
between us is over,
i walk
the streets
of Hayward by myself
at night,
wishing
cars would
hit me as I crossed
the streets
but, they always honked,
or I was yelled out to
by some random Bay Area adult
saving me,
but, also cursing at me
asking me
"don't you know better?"

the question haunts me today
as I continue to ask myself
every day I hope he'll call again like before,
"don't you know better?"

our story was so fast
the part you played
was like a tornado
blowing me into an
oblivion of allure
i've never felt.
you were here
and then
you were gone.
i am going mad
thinking this whole thing
was only me dreaming
all along.

i was just short-term
comfort.
i was just seasonal,
summer.

silly girl
tricked
by cupids' arrow
once again.

i don't understand what happened,
why god would play
such a cruel joke on me?
what did I do
to deserve such pain?

there is no vaccination
for my new ideas
of freedom.

there is no cure
for decaying love that has
been planted
into a naïve heart.

palms around my neck,
strangulation,
are looping words from your tongue,
suffocating me
with a burning reality,
leaving bruises on my ego
with aloneness,
despairing my mind,
waiting to hear him again,
but, I'm fading to the silence

he visits me
in my dreams
and even in my dreams
he runs away from me.

i held on to him
for months
and he embraced
me repeatedly.
telling me
exactly what I
wanted to hear,
telling me
he felt the
same way,
but, his
actions
told me
the opposite.
told me I
wasn't who
he wanted
to be with.
told me
he didn't feel
the same way,
leaving me alone
to create stories
and piece together
the insanity alone.

and now,
i want my heart back,
i'll do whatever it takes.

the barrier that he broke
surrounding it,
he stole with grace.

left with it in his pocket.
he wears it on a necklace these days
like a grand token of achievement
like some prize.

but,
i'm incomplete without my heart
i'm numb to the world around me
the demons just fill my empty spaces
with horrible fictitious memories.

i felt it
it was sloppy
and messy
but, it was ours,
it was our chaotic love story.

now, it's gone,
slipped away in the night
like it was never here
and I feel I could die

part four
soul's madness

i sit by myself
next to an ocean,
wondering why
he chose another woman,

wondering how he
could look me in the eyes
and tell me he wanted me in
his life,
only to disappear
and leave my heart in
a purgatory of confusion.

he
is
a living poetry,
on the verge of monster
on the brink of demonically
possessing my soul
with sadness

the moment
i realized
i could never be
the her to his we
i lost myself
down the road
of the
unrequited
lover's lunacy

i wish
i had known
who I was
dealing with.
i wish I could have
known his
weather
forecast
was
snow flaky

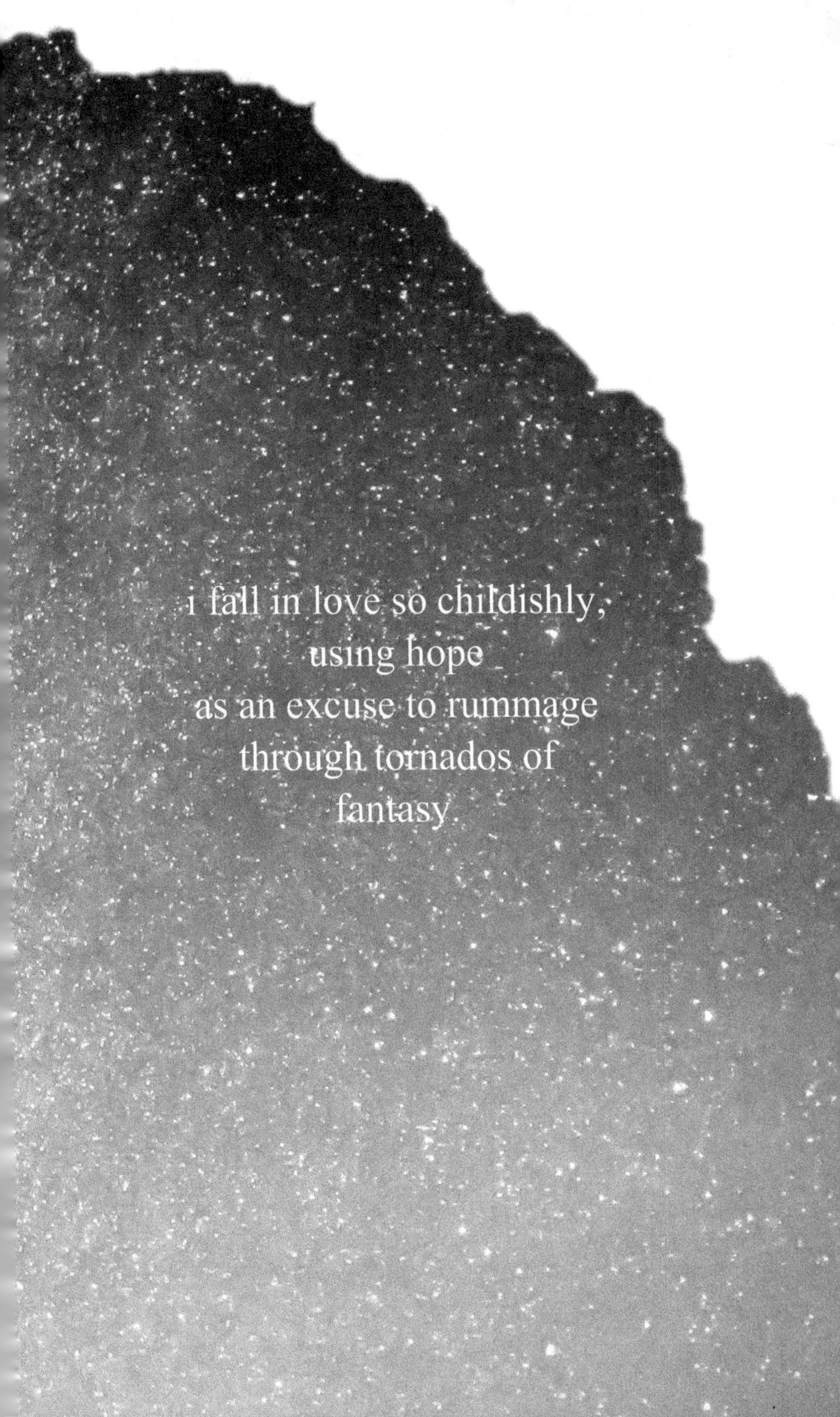

i fall in love so childishly,
using hope
as an excuse to rummage
through tornados of
fantasy.

his eyes were
blue symmetry,
two ponds of grace
staring into my soul,
they were white lace
draping over
my heart,
burying me
into his grave,
a sadistic death.

love
is
patient
love
is kind
so, I
waited
i was
blind.

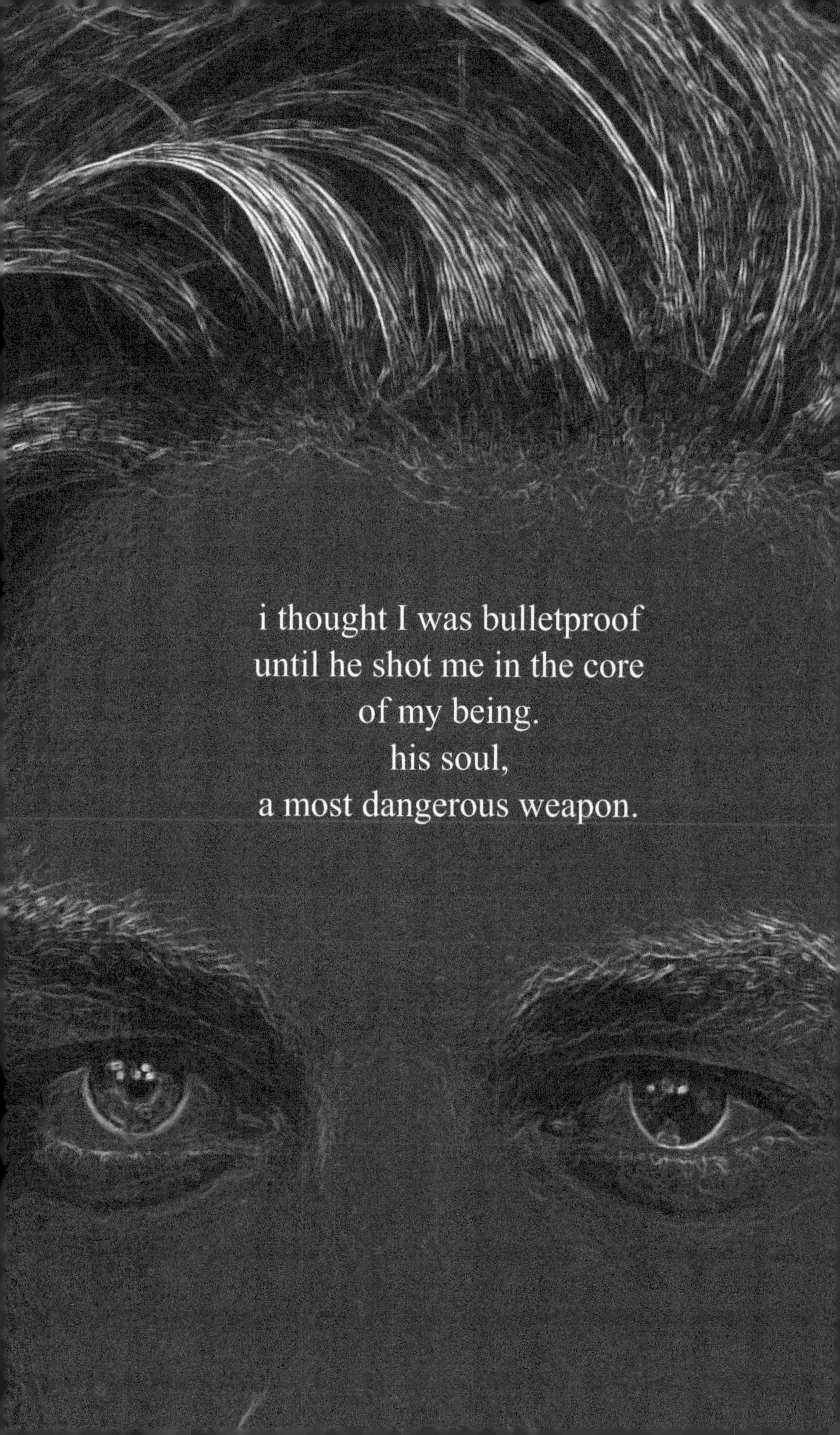

i thought I was bulletproof
until he shot me in the core
of my being.
his soul,
a most dangerous weapon.

i feel helpless
to my hopeful heart.

i
never knew why people
called it
heart
break.
now I know.
i feel broken,
like all the pieces of my life
i spent years building,
figuring out,
were starting to make sense,
and then he came in
like a tornado,
shattering the pieces
before spinning off,
leaving me broken and empty.
leaving my life as
a blank canvas again.

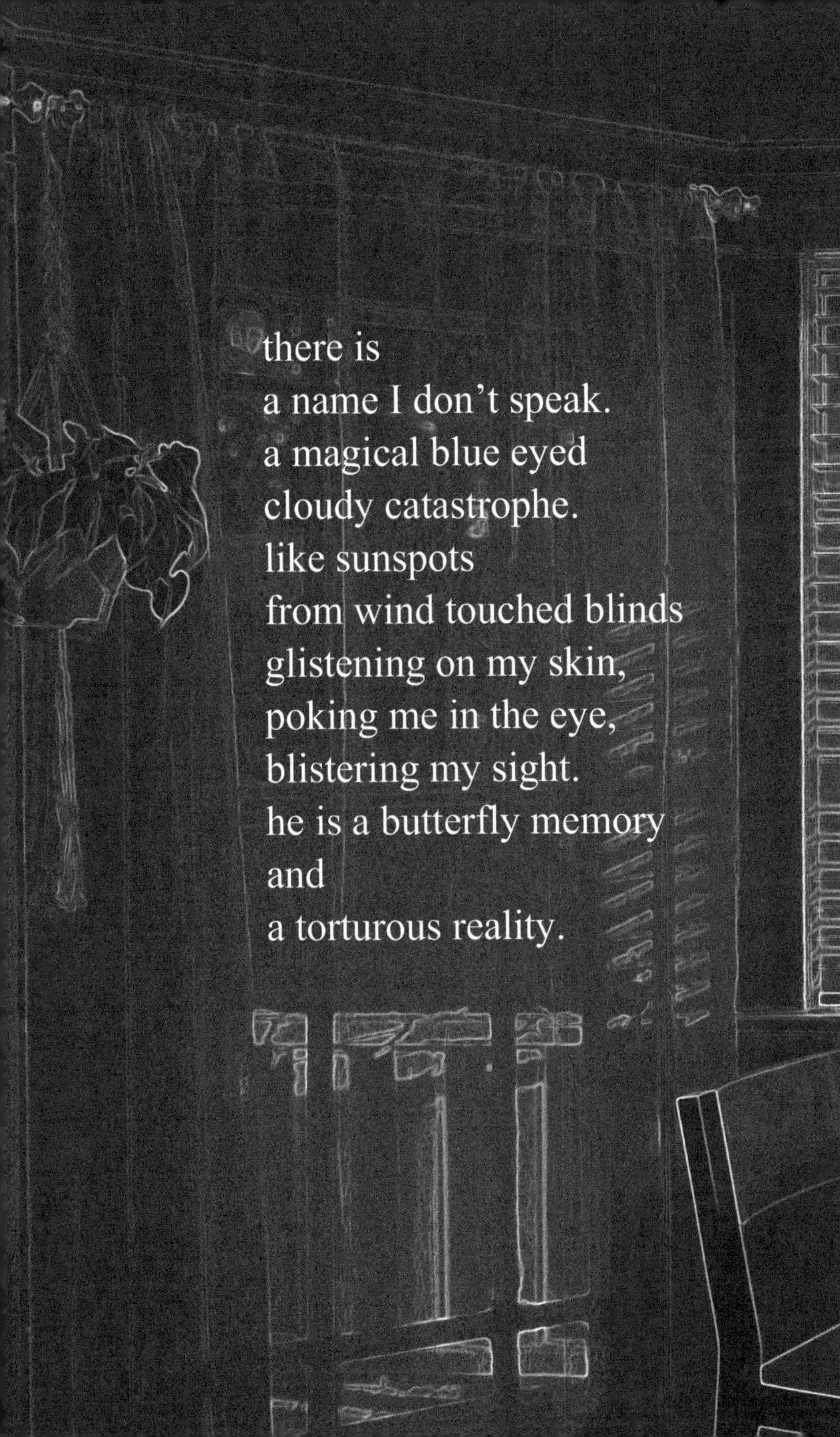

there is
a name I don't speak.
a magical blue eyed
cloudy catastrophe.
like sunspots
from wind touched blinds
glistening on my skin,
poking me in the eye,
blistering my sight.
he is a butterfly memory
and
a torturous reality.

i rip the petals
off this flower
one by one.
i tell myself
with each pull,
he loves me not
he loves me
hoping to end on
he loves me,
realizing
i've spent days
ripping apart
beautiful flowers
just to feed
my heart lies.

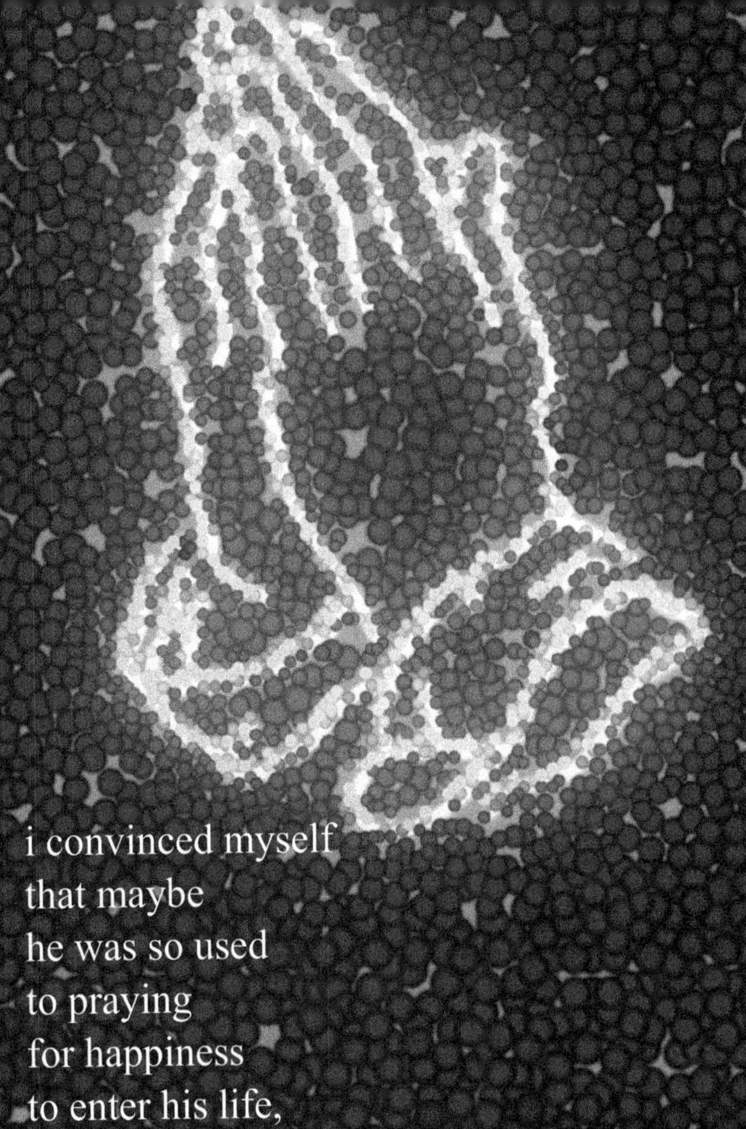

i convinced myself
that maybe
he was so used
to praying
for happiness
to enter his life,
that when it did
he ran away from her
because
he was too used to the ugliness
and sadness of life.
i was wrong.

i always
thought he
would come
back around
but,
that's the thing
with one-way streets,
they are not meant
to turn back round.

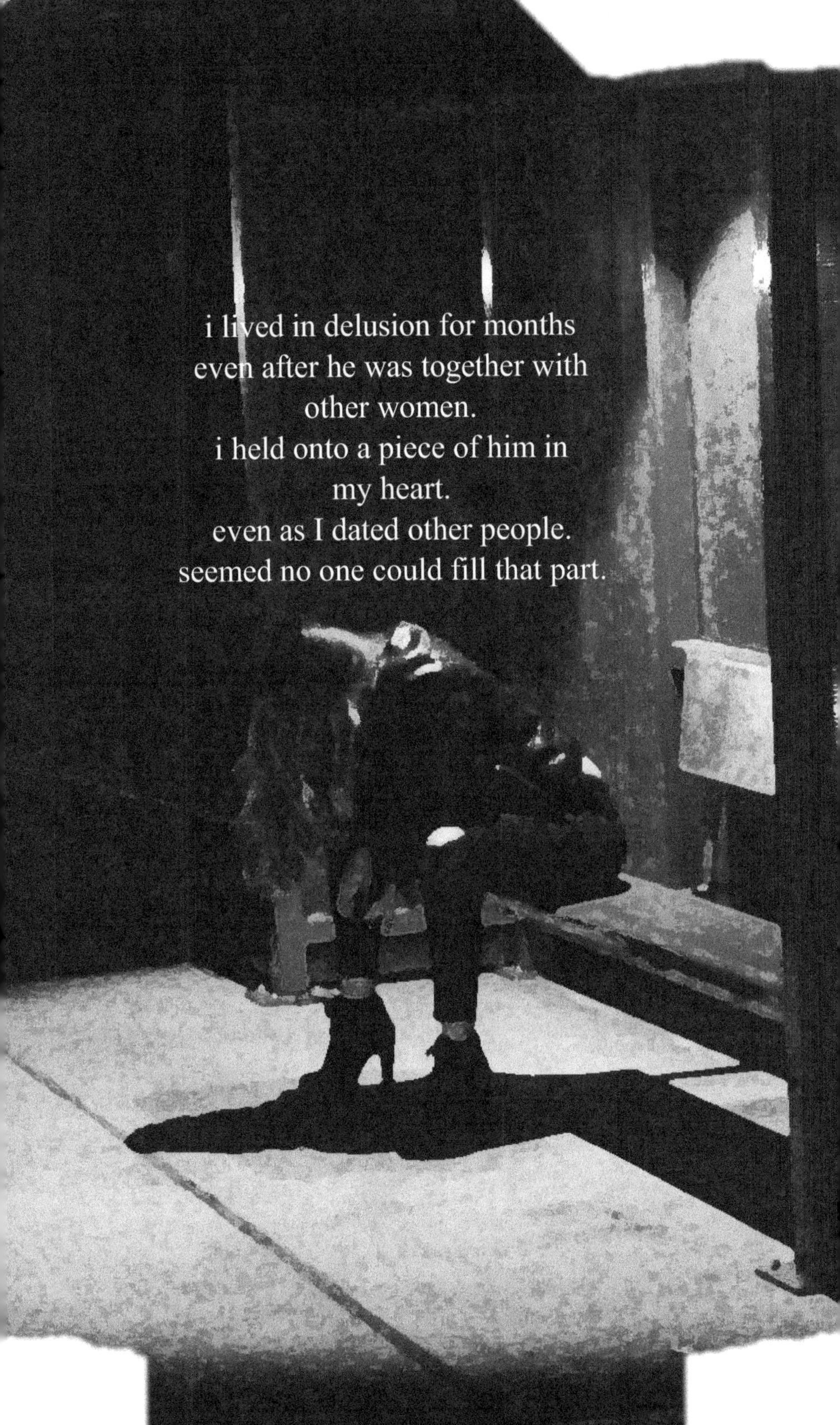

i lived in delusion for months
even after he was together with
other women.
i held onto a piece of him in
my heart.
even as I dated other people.
seemed no one could fill that part.

pharmaceutical
love
he was my therapy
now,
a distant remedy
that I can't reach,
just a memory,
and my heart
becomes inflamed,
a never healing blister
bubbling with puss,
bleeding through
my chest
is to be without him
is to know an endless wound
is to be trapped in
a loveless world
is to be imprisoned in
reminiscence
of an
existent
medicinal
assistance.

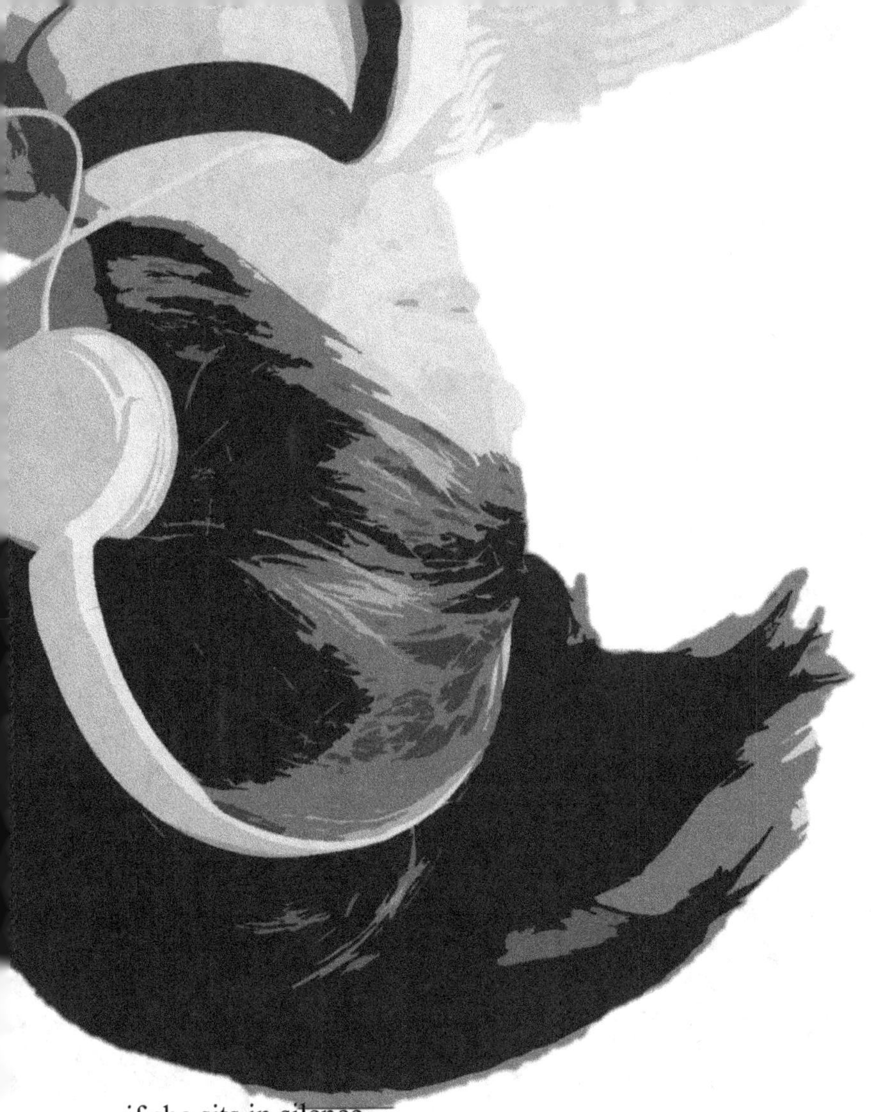

if she sits in silence
for too long,
she can't breathe.
she can't stop the tears.
so, she plays loud music,
with loud bass
to drown away the sounds of
her heart pounding out of her chest

she keeps
yelling at herself in the mirror.
slapping her face with cold water.
tired of sucking on fake love,
tired of feeling like a monster,
tired of being this
vampiric formation,
tired of hearing
this horrible repeated song
"I don't want you"
Please, god,
change the station.

i cried today
with black sunglasses on
in the middle
of Bay Area rush hour traffic,
letting salty water drops
sprinkle all over my cheeks and chin
at the thought
of him finding a more beautiful woman
to complete him.

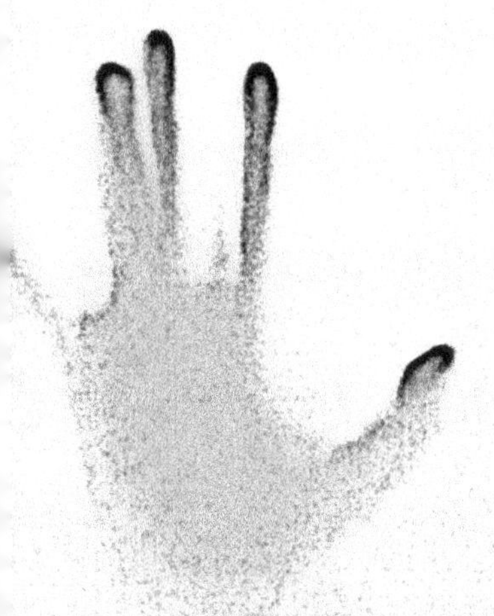

you know you've fallen in love alone
when the texts you write to him
have nowhere to be sent
because
you've deleted him from your phone
and you've
deleted him from every
possible social media outlet you could
find him on,
and then you've blocked him on
everything.

you know you've fallen in love alone
because you've disconnected
every possible connection
to reach out to him
so, he can't reject you once more
with silence
or with *read*.

it feels empty
laying on this bench alone
staring at the ocean,
staring at San Francisco,
the skies are so blue
and though the water sparkles
a poetic indigo sea.
i know
i am in captivity
from diving too deep into
unsafe emotional waters
since I can't enjoy the beauty
before me.
my mind shows me
the scenes of us.
a tragic, confusing story
of love touching me
and feeling life
rip it away.

i sit a lot at my desk
and I feel my hands
creep over my face
at the thoughts
of the past.

i am ashamed
of the reality
of falling in…
alone.
i can't even say it.

i tell myself,
at least
i had the courage to
accept my feelings of him.

i tell myself
i forgive him
for running away,

i forgive him for
stringing someone
like me along.

someone who
carries
unearned loyalty
around on a leash,

someone who
decides
to see the good
in people,
even when they
don't deserve it,
I forgive him

the silence is
the worst part.
the most dreadful truth,
listening to my
own thoughts
hearing my own,
words
never spoken,
feeling them die
from deep within
the rivers of my heart.
the ones that
were meant
to flow to him,
disintegrating
each by each
into
nothingness.

her heart
created a solitary
confining loyalty to him
no one could free her from.

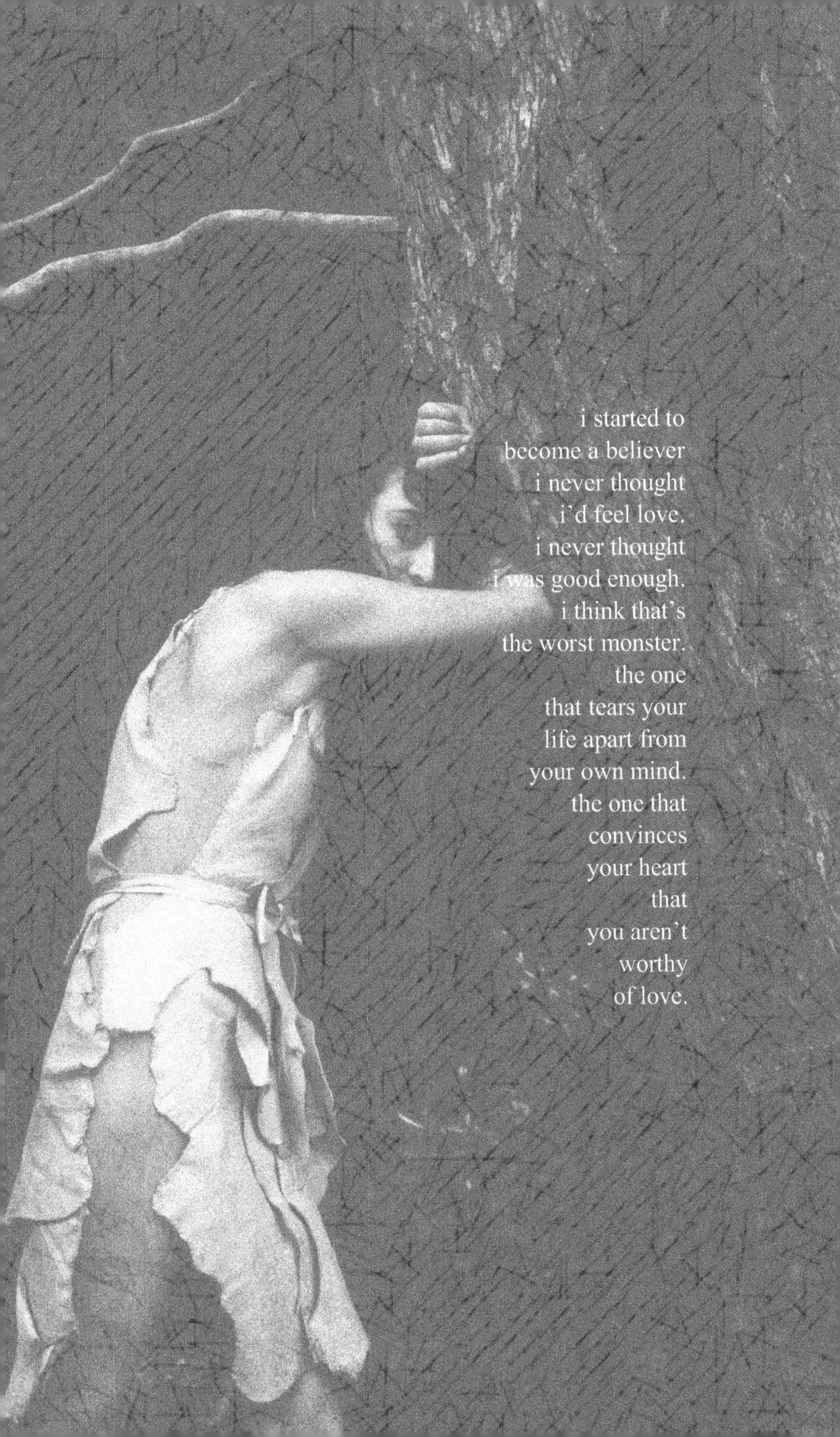

i started to
become a believer
i never thought
i'd feel love.
i never thought
i was good enough.
i think that's
the worst monster.
the one
that tears your
life apart from
your own mind.
the one that
convinces
your heart
that
you aren't
worthy
of love.

i am a soft rose
blooming to the sun
awaiting a refreshing
rainstorm
to wash your memory from
my petals.

when woman falls in love,
wolf inside emerges
from the caves deep within.
she becomes monster for love.
howling at the moon for love.
dying to protect for love.

long beyond
their seed of passion
hath planted,
when they hugged me
goodbye forever,
a disgusting repetitive motion,
twice in a row it happened,
and after I thought her torment
left me for good,
his torment snuck
upon my body,
a sort of rotten fragrance
crept into my spirit.
i discovered his hidden
attachment to me
fermented into my gut,
preserving in the depths
of my very cells,
becoming a bacterium,
decaying my womb,
pinching every
nerve in my back,
weakening my legs so
i could not walk,
rapidly spreading,
multiplying as
a most awful disease,
crawling through my veins,
collapsing one lung at a time,
reaching my heart,
blocking both arteries
into the worst kind of pain,
a slow death caused by unrequited love.

DOWN THE RABBIT HOLE

i wonder if I will
make it out of this madness alive.

i wish people
left my heart
as easy as they
left my life.

part five

soul's wisdom

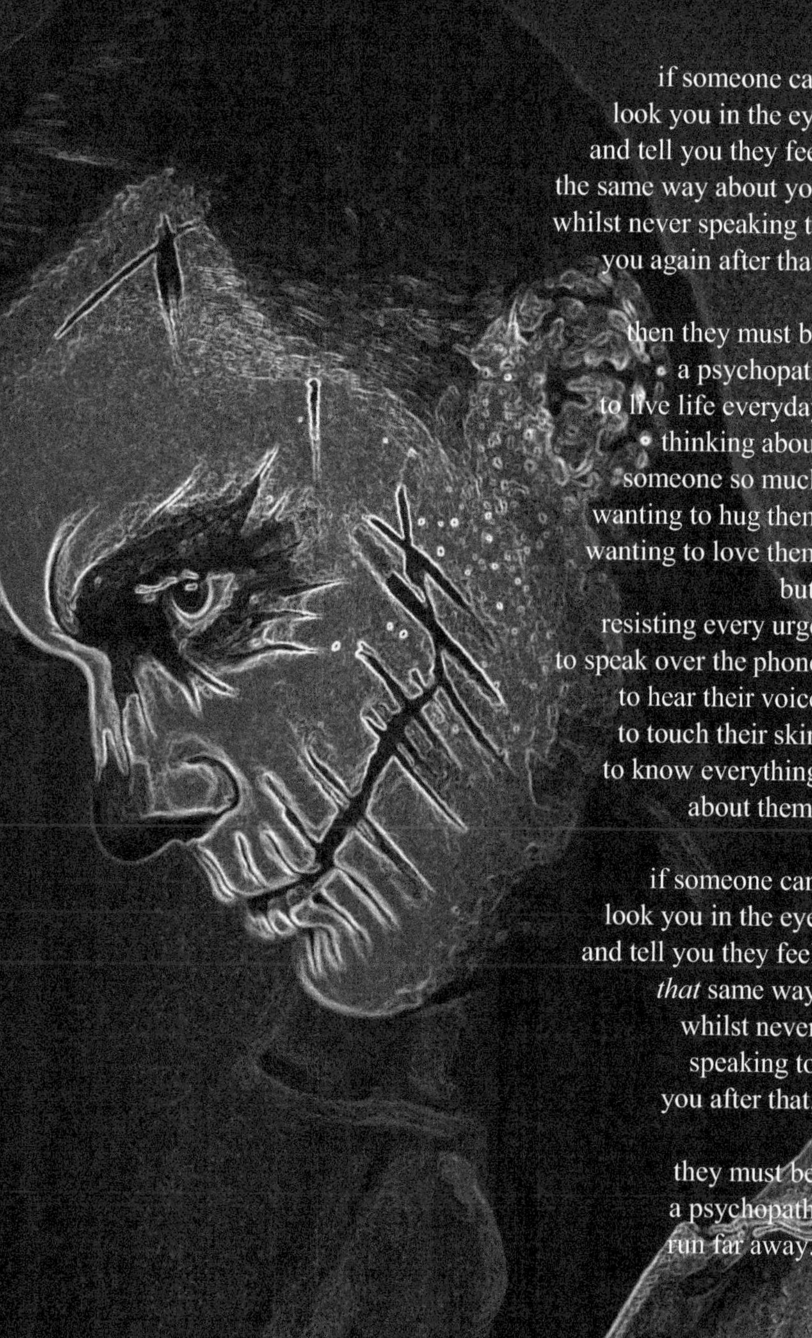

if someone can
look you in the eye
and tell you they feel
the same way about you
whilst never speaking to
you again after that,

then they must be
a psychopath
to live life everyday
thinking about
someone so much
wanting to hug them
wanting to love them
but,
resisting every urge
to speak over the phone
to hear their voice
to touch their skin
to know everything
about them.

if someone can
look you in the eye
and tell you they feel
that same way
whilst never
speaking to
you after that,

they must be
a psychopath
run far away.

don't lose yourself
trying to entice someone
else to love you
in ways they could never
live up to.

don't be fooled by the song
they share with you,
telling you,
this reminds me of you
and it's some sort of
fantasy.
love is a fantastic reality.
it is real
it is not just a fantasy.

if you care about someone truly,
tell them you don't feel for them as you used to
instead of disappearing into silence.
set them free.

"the timing was never right"
is the quote that
ends or begins
relationships.
most of the time,
it ends them.

it's not their fault
they couldn't fall in love with
you.

it's not my fault
that I fell in love with him.

it's no one's fault
who they fall in love with.

you should know
your worth
is more important
than letting anyone
treat you as second
string
if you're treating
them
as if they are first
team.

good friends
who listen,
who hug
you when
you cry,
who are
still friends
after months
of hearing you
go on and on
about someone
are a rare
blessing.
thank them
for helping
to save your life.

love is a mysterious
creature that knows
no boundaries.
It lurks in the
spirits of the lonely,
settles in the souls
of the honest,
makes its homes in
whoever is somber
enough, or happy
enough,
it doesn't wait
for who
has planned
everything right,
it doesn't wait
for who is ready.
it stampedes
onto hearts
and stomps on
whatever stands
in the way
of its wrath.

never wait for anyone to call.
if you must,
throw your phone over a cliff
but,
never wait for someone to call.

don't get
used to
wishing
for rain
to bring
you
rainbows.
don't get
used to
wishing
for
storms
to bring
you
beauty.

love
is not
something to chase.
love is something
to build.

don't
tell her
you feel the
same way,
if you can
sleep in bed
next to
another
name.

don't use hope as a
catalyst to fall in love,
use loyalty.

you can't be
mad at someone
you fall in love with
who is mad at
themselves,
who is mad at the
world.

you can't be sad
over someone who
you fall in love with
who is sad over
themselves,
who is sad over the
world.

you can only be mad
at yourself.

you can only be sad
over yourself.

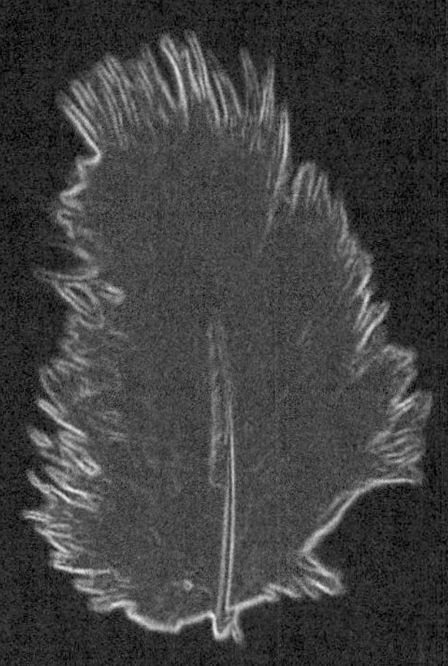

maybe,
he treated you so bad
because he knew
he didn't deserve you
and for that
thank him.
now, you can find
what you
truly deserve.

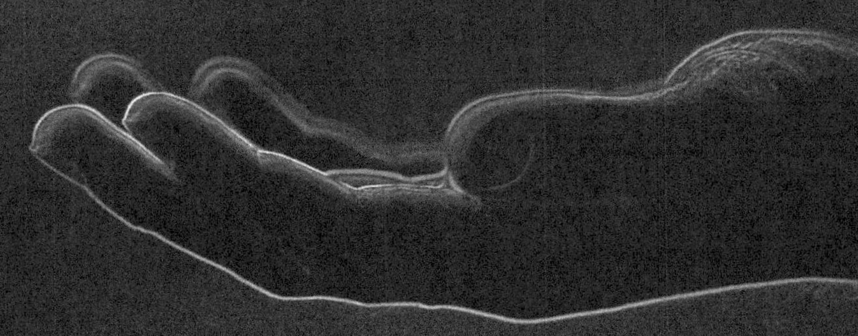

when he told me, I was *everything*
i knew it would never work out.
i knew I could never truly
let someone in
who believed in me so much.
and the moment I allowed myself to
feel for him,
my heart slapped me in the face.
he started to feel like
everything
the very instant when we became
nothing.

life is a quest for the willing
lust is a quest for the adventurous
love is a quest for the courageous
loss is a quest for the human

build
your
chapters
based on
truth.
don't
build
their story
based
on
hope.

I needed closure
and I needed healing.
the words just poured out of me
onto these pages
and somehow, I still feel
overwhelmed with words to say.

i never needed
you to love me.
i needed me
to love me.

i look back now
and understand
the fleeting meanings
of my words
to him.
when something *is not* said
nothing is all that exists.
when something *is* said
nothing can still
be all that exists.
for he was never
meant to hear the words
pouring out of my heart
he was never
meant to accept my love
it was not in his script
to play that part

don't try to save someone
who needs spiritual revelation.
that's bigger than all of us,
that's not the role any of us are
supposed to play.

if three or more people
say the same thing about
your relations with
someone
you love
which is
leave
never talk to them again
let them go
it might benefit you
to listen to them.

never wait on someone
to come around again.
if they left once,
they'll leave again.

don't stop living your life
when you realize
they don't feel the same way.

don't stop loving yourself
when you realize
they don't feel the same way.

don't stop believing in love
when you realize
they don't feel the same way.

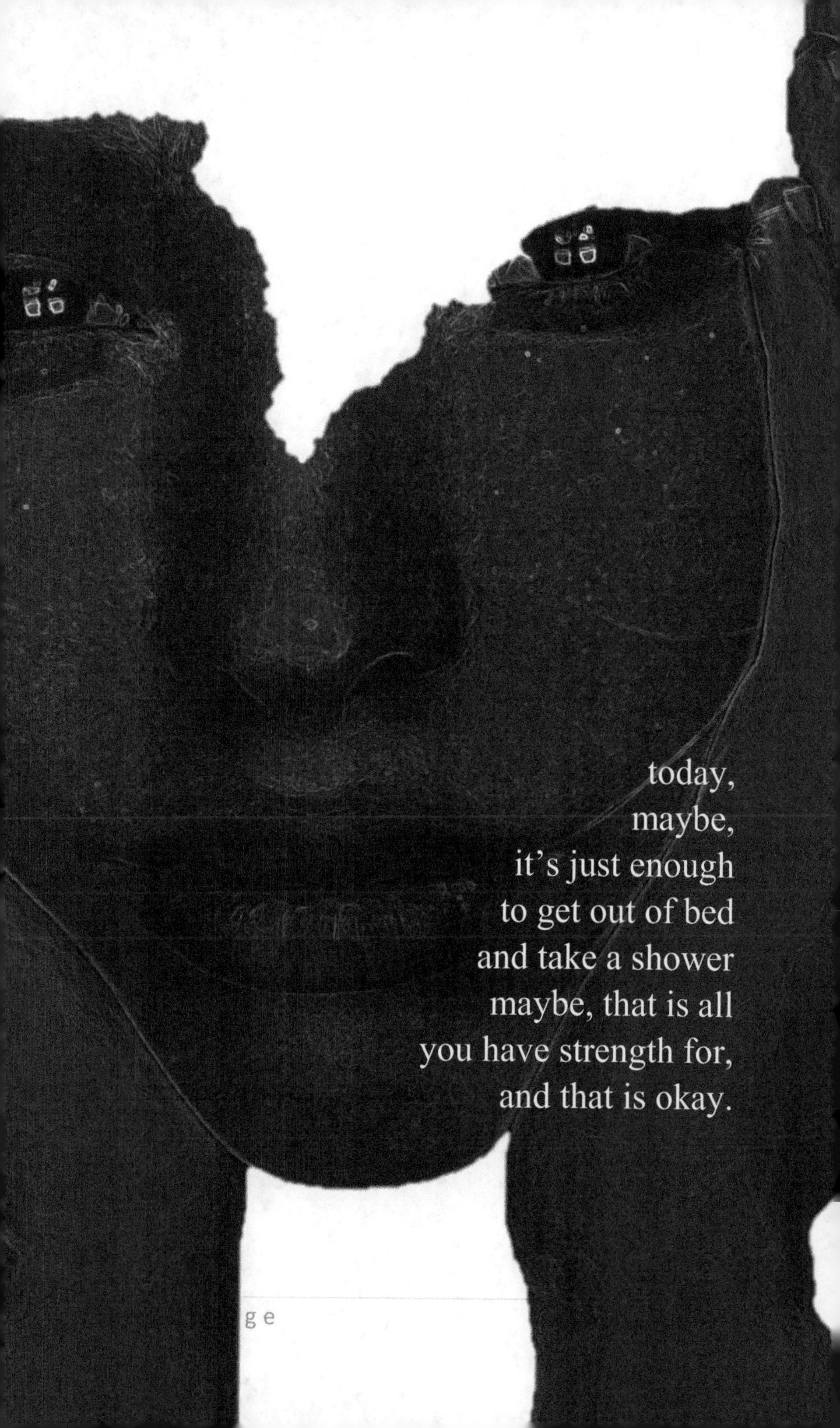

today,
maybe,
it's just enough
to get out of bed
and take a shower
maybe, that is all
you have strength for,
and that is okay.

if you have to cry,
cry,
if you have to scream,
scream,
if you have to cry and scream
over and over again,
do it,
you'll feel better after.

restore your mind in silence.
renew your body in peace.
revitalize your soul in serene places.

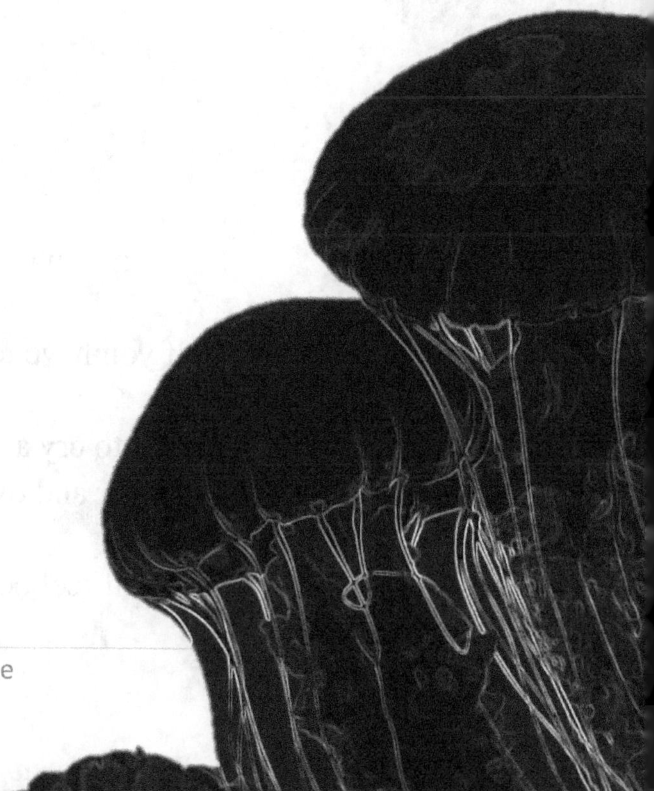

sometimes,
things just don't work out
and maybe,
that's a blessing in disguise.

it was never love,
it was intense attraction,
it was only passion.

there is no time limit
to recovering from
unrequited love.
don't let the world
fool you
into thinking there is
some kind of
instant remedy
for this wound.

let yourself
breakdown,
let yourself reflect,
let yourself go,
pull yourself back
together,
workout,
eat healthy,
eat junk food,
learn to be okay
by yourself
one day at a time.

darling,
it aint ever foolish to fall in love.
it's courageous,
it's beautiful,
it's wonderous,
it's magnificent.

i sat in my room one night
and I felt this stinging in my heart,
this open wound inside
asking me to make a new choice,
begging me to change my decision,
"let go of them, please".

so, I listened
i finally listened.
i let them go.
all of the he's and she's I loved alone,
and it felt like a huge knife
was pulled out of my soul.
i felt relieved
from a pressure
never meant to
live within me.

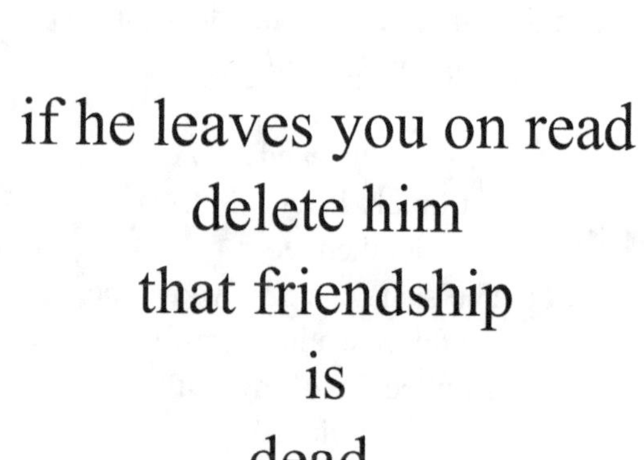

if he leaves you on read
delete him
that friendship
is
dead.

fake love
highlights
the holes in your heart.

real love
mends the holes
in your heart.

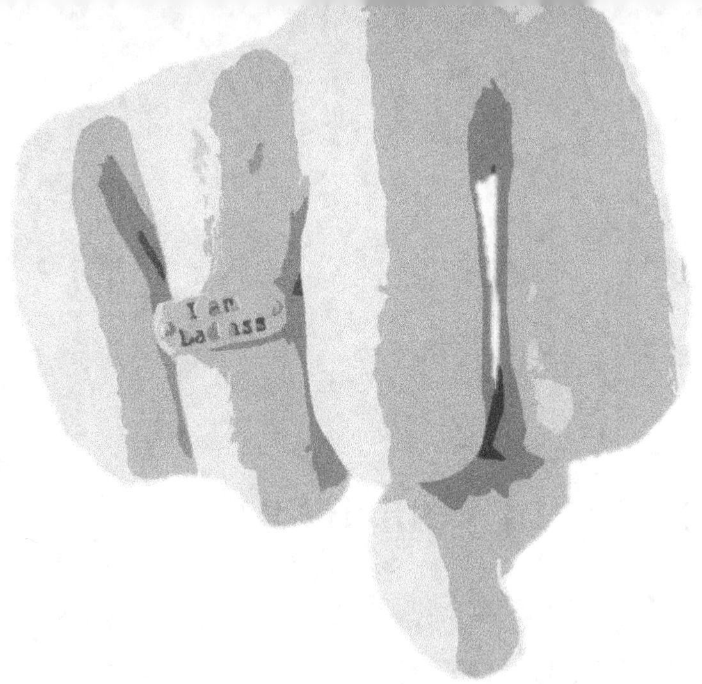

they made a choice,
now
it's your turn.
make a choice
to love who you are
and every time
you look in the mirror
accept that
you deserve the best,
you deserve a loving partner,
you deserve a healthy life.

i finally understood.
he was a catalyst
shining a light on
a deeper wound
inside me,
in existence
before he
appeared.

for that,
i thank him.

maybe it's not so bad
after all,

maybe,
it is the perfect time
to fall in love alone